Contents

What is a mythical creature?

Stories from all around the world tell us about **mythical** creatures. They are monsters and magical beings that many people believed in. Do you think they could be real?

DID YOU KNOW?
People tell **myths** about dragons in Europe, Asia, Australia, and North and South America.

Mermaids

Charlotte Guillain

www.raintreepublishers.co.uk
Visit our website to find out more information about Raintree books.

To order:
☎ Phone 0845 6044371
🖷 Fax +44 (0) 1865 312263
🖳 Email myorders@raintreepublishers.co.uk

Customers from outside the UK please telephone +44 1865 312262

Raintree is an imprint of Capstone Global Library Limited, a company incorporated in England and Wales having its registered office at 7 Pilgrim Street, London, EC4V 6LB – Registered company number: 6695582

Text © Capstone Global Library Limited 2011
First published in hardback in 2011
Paperback edition first published in 2012
The moral rights of the proprietor have been asserted.

Edited by Adrian Vigliano, Rebecca Rissman, and Nancy Dickmann
Designed by Joanna Hinton Malivoire
Levelling by Jeanne Clidas
Original illustrations by Christian Slade
Original illustrations © Capstone Global Library
Picture research by Elizabeth Alexander
Production by Victoria Fitzgerald
Originated by Capstone Global Library
Printed and bound in China by CTPS

ISBN 978 1 4062 1645 5 (hardback)
14 13 12 11 10
10 9 8 7 6 5 4 3 2 1

ISBN 978 1 4062 2034 6 (paperback)
15 14 13 12 11
10 9 8 7 6 5 4 3 2 1

British Library Cataloguing in Publication Data
Guillain, Charlotte.
Mermaids. -- (Mythical creatures)
398.4'5-dc22
A full catalogue record for this book is available from the British Library.

Acknowledgements
We would like to thank the following for permission to reproduce photographs: akg-images p. **8** (John William Waterhouse/Royal Academy of Fine Arts); Alamy pp. **9** (© United Archives GmbH), **11** (© Lee Foster), **14** (© Niday Picture Library), **20** (© Black Star), **23** (© Bryan & Cherry Alexander Photography), **29** (© Chris A Crumley); American Museum of Natural History Library p. **21**; © Andrice Arp p. **19**; Corbis pp. **10** (© Sea World of California), **28** (© Stephen Frink); Sawaki Suushi p. **25**; The Bridgeman Art Library p. **12** (© Christie's Images).

Every effort has been made to contact copyright holders of material reproduced in this book. Any omissions will be rectified in subsequent printings if notice is given to the publisher.

Disclaimer
All the Internet addresses (URLs) given in this book were valid at the time of going to press. However, due to the dynamic nature of the Internet, some addresses may have changed, or sites may have changed or ceased to exist since publication. While the author and publisher regret any inconvenience this may cause readers, no responsibility for any such changes can be accepted by either the author or the publisher.

Some words are shown in bold, **like this**. You can find out what they mean by looking in the glossary.

Have you heard stories about fairies?
Do you think they could be real?

What is a mermaid?

People in many countries tell stories about mermaids. They have the head and body of a human and the tail of a fish or other sea animal. **Myths** tell us about sailors seeing mermaids from their ships. There are many pictures, songs, and stories about mermaids.

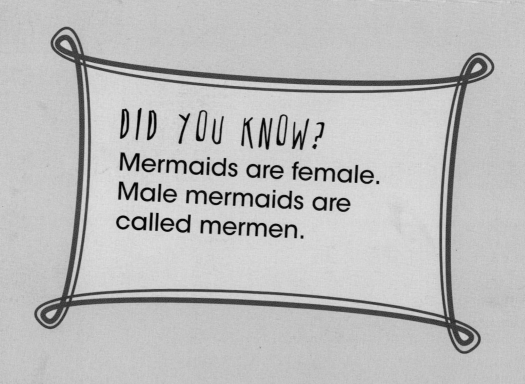

DID YOU KNOW?
Mermaids are female. Male mermaids are called mermen.

7

Myths tell us mermaids are beautiful. Mermaids live underwater, but they can sometimes be seen on rocks. A few myths say mermaids come onto land and pretend to be humans.

DID YOU KNOW?

The Little Mermaid is a famous story about a mermaid who falls in love with a human prince.

The mermaid myth

Mermaid **myths** may have started when travellers saw strange animals in the sea. Sailors saw creatures they had never seen before and made up stories. Some people think sailors saw manatees in the Caribbean Sea and thought they were mermaids.

manatee

11

Mermaids of Europe

One Ancient Greek **myth** is about a great leader's sister, Thessalonike (say *thess-ah-lo-nee-kay*). She turned into a mermaid when she died. She asked sailors a question and drowned them if they gave the wrong answer.

Ancient Greek mermaid

Europe

Greece

Thessalonike

13

Christopher Columbus

Sailors from Europe started many mermaid stories. Christopher Columbus thought he saw three mermaids near Haiti in 1493. He said they were "not as pretty" as the mermaids he had seen in pictures.

DID YOU KNOW?
The explorer John Smith said that he saw a mermaid with a fish's tail, round eyes, and long green hair.

Mermaids of Asia

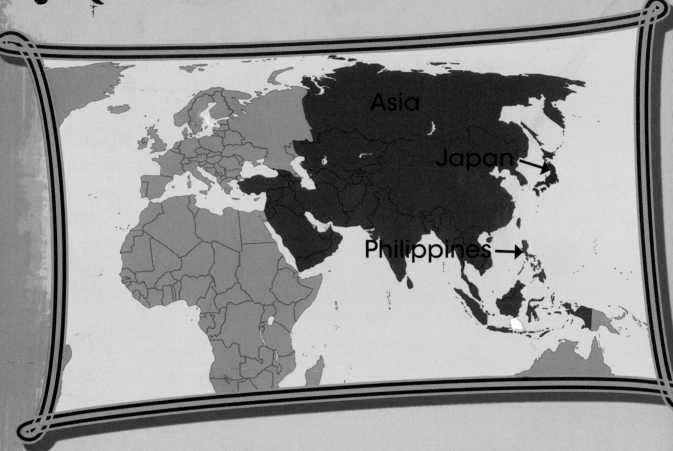

In many Asian countries, people tell stories about mermaids. Mermaids in the Philippines are called Sirena (say *seh-rain-ah*). **Myths** say that they sing and **hypnotize** sailors. Then they take the sailors under the sea as gifts to the gods.

Sirena

Siyokoy

DID YOU KNOW?

Mermen in the Phillipines are called Siyokoy (*say sho-koy*). Some stories say they have long, green **tentacles**. They drown humans for food.

17

In Japan people told stories of the Ningyo (say *ning-yo*). This was a fish with a human head that sang like a bird. Ningyo could bring good or bad luck.

DID YOU KNOW?
Some people thought it was lucky to eat a Ningyo. But fishermen did not want to catch a Ningyo as it would bring storms and bad luck.

Mermaids of Africa and the Caribbean

Slaves from Africa took mermaid **myths** to the Caribbean. Mami Wata (say *ma-mee wah-tah*) has a woman's head and a body with a fish or snake's tail. Stories say this water **spirit** can heal ill people. But if she is angry, she drowns humans.

Mami Wata

Caribbean

Africa

Lasirèn

DID YOU KNOW?

Myths about Lasirèn (say *la-see-REN*) tell about a Caribbean water spirit who takes humans under the sea and brings them back with special powers.

Mermaids of North America

Inuit people in North America tell stories about Sedna (say *SHED-nah*). This **myth** says a man threw his daughter into the sea and she became Sedna. The story says she is half fish and half human.

North America

Inuit Sedna carving

DID YOU KNOW?
Some Sedna stories say the father chopped off his daughter's fingers and they became whales, seals, and walruses.

Close relatives

There are many other **mythical** creatures that live underwater. Australian **aboriginal** people tell stories of yawkyawks (say *yahk-yahks*) in **waterholes**. People say that the long weed in waterholes could be a yawkyawk's hair.

DID YOU KNOW?

Japanese **myths** tell about these sea monsters:

- Ushi-oni (say *ooh-shee-oh-nee*) has a body like a spider or crab.
- Nure-onna (say *new-ree-oh-nah*) has the head of a woman and the body of a snake.

Nure-onna

Could mermaids exist?

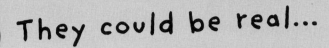 **They could be real...**

- People all over the world tell stories about mermaids.

✗ **I'm not so sure...**

- These stories may have spread around the world as sailors travelled.

✓ **They could be real...**

- Some people say they have found dead mermaids washed up on the beach.

✗ **I'm not so sure...**

- Dead mermaids turn out to be **hoaxes**. Nobody has ever found a real mermaid.

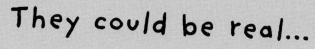

✓ They could be real...

- Some parts of the ocean are very deep. We don't know if mermaids are living there or not.

● I'm not so sure...

- Scientists have found many creatures living in deep oceans, but they have never found **evidence** of a mermaid.

There are many interesting stories about mermaids. What do you think?

Reality versus myth

Manatee (real)

Found: around Florida and the Caribbean and the Amazon River

Lives: in the sea near the coast and in rivers

Likes: to eat plants and play with other manatees

Seen: very rarely. The manatee is an **endangered** animal.

Mermaid (myth)

Found: all over the world

Lives: under the sea

Likes: to comb hair and sing to sailors

Seen: in films and art from around the world.

Glossary

aboriginal first people living in Australia

endangered in danger of dying out

evidence facts that tell us if something is true

hoax trick

hypnotize put someone into a sleeplike state

myth traditional story, often about magical creatures and events

mythical found in myths

slave person who is the property of another person and is forced to work. At one time many slaves were brought to North America and the Caribbean from Africa.

spirit magical creature

tentacle long, bendable body part of an animal such as an octopus

waterhole natural well or pond

Find out more

Books

Stories of Mermaids, Russell Punter
(Usborne Books, 2009)

The Little Mermaid, Hans Christian Andersen,
adapted by Naomi Lewis (Walker Books, 2009)

*The Orchard Book of the Unicorn and Other
Magical Animals*, Margaret Mayo
(Orchard Books, 2008)

Websites

http://greece.mrdonn.org/myths.html
The Ancient Greeks told many stories about
mythical creatures. This website has a collection
of these stories that you can read online.

http://hca.gilead.org.il
Go to this website to read about Hans Christian
Andersen, the author of *The Little Mermaid.* You
can read some of his stories here as well.

Index